CINCO de MAYO

Yesterday and Today

Text and design copyright © 1996 by Maria Cristina Urrutia and Rebeca Orozco
Translation copyright © 1999 by Groundwood Books Ltd.
Originally published in Mexico as *La Batalla del 5 de Mayo: ayer y hoy* by Ediciones Tecolote 1996
First English-language edition 1999
First paperback edition 2002
New paperback edition 2008

Groundwood Books / House of Anansi Press
110 Spadina Avenue, Suite 801, Toronto, Ontario M5V 2K4
Distributed in the USA by Publishers Group West
1700 Fourth Street, Berkeley, CA 94710

Library and Archives Canada Cataloguing in Publication
Urrutia, Ma. Cristina (María Cristina)
Cinco de Mayo : yesterday and today / authored by Maria Cristina Urrutia and Rebeca Orozco.
Translation of: La batalla del 5 de Mayo : ayer y hoy.
ISBN-13: 978-0-88899-877-4
ISBN-10: 0-88899-877-5
1. Mexico–History–European intervention, 1861-1867–Juvenile literature. 2. Cinco de Mayo, Battle of, Puebla, Mexico, 1862–Juvenile literature. 3. Cinco de Mayo (Mexican holiday)–Juvenile literature.
I. Orozco, Rebeca II. Title.
F1233.U7713 2008   j972'.07   C2007-907131-7

Printed and bound in China

I speak of what I know. Also of what I have seen and what I have lived. History should not be dead. That is why, every year on the fifth of May, the Cinco de Mayo, my father, my son and I, and all our village, too, reenact the battle of Puebla. We dress up as Mexicans and Frenchmen. We act out our parts. And here, in San Miguel Tlaixpan, we celebrate a very important day in the history of our country, Mexico.

CINCO de MAYO

Yesterday and Today

Text and design by Maria Cristina Urrutia and Rebeca Orozco

GROUNDWOOD BOOKS / HOUSE OF ANANSI PRESS

TORONTO BERKELEY

"Why did we fight the French?" ask the children as we dress them up for the Cinco de Mayo festival.

"We fought for our freedom and to defend our land from a foreign emperor. The French broke all the treaties we had signed and sent eight war ships to invade us, pretending to collect on a debt."

The French landed in Veracruz and marched toward Puebla. They carried heavy weapons. Many of them died from the heat and yellow fever.

But on they came. The Mexican army awaited them high on Guadalupe Hill overlooking the city of Puebla.

Let the bells ring!
In our village we build
Guadalupe Hill right in
the central square. It is
made of wooden beams, ash
tree branches and maguey flowers.
We fortify it and prepare for battle. We climb up, we climb down
to the tune of the chirimia whistle and the teponatzli drum.

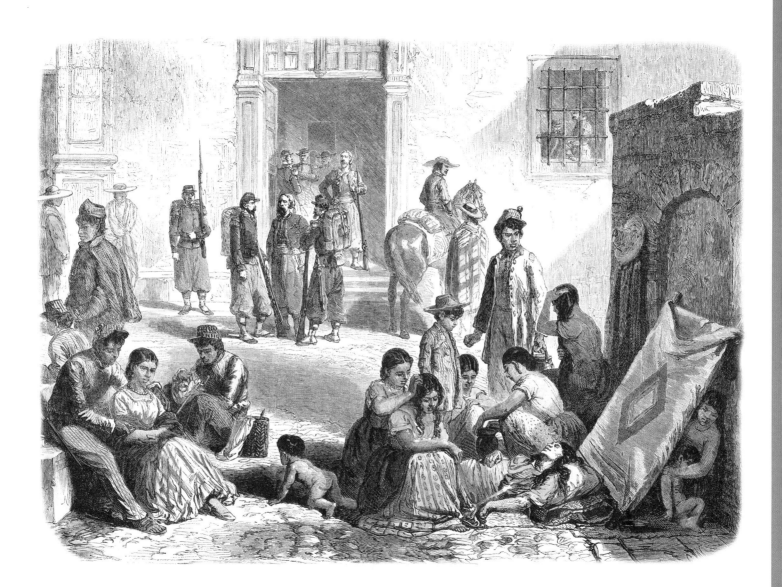

The French soldiers were bearded and strong. Their blue jackets were covered with medals they had won in combat, and their baggy pantaloons were red. The knapsacks on their backs had biscuits and bread in them, and even shiny coffee pots.

In our village the actors who play the French also wear red and blue. They carry flags and make-believe rifles and guns.

The Mexican army had help on that long-ago day. Chinacos, whose courage had no bounds, were experts with lances, sabres and machetes.

Everyone in our village wants to play a Chinaco because they get to ride on horseback and chase down the French until they are captured.

Other important allies were the Zacapoaxtle Indians. They fought on foot with machetes.

If you want to be a Zacapoaxtle in our village you must wear cotton pantaloons, leather thong sandals and straw hats. Paint your face with charcoal and carry string bags with tortillas and nopal cactus. Be proud to fight under General Juan Francisco. An Indian queen called La Naca comes with us.

The story goes that when it was time for battle, the French dropped their knapsacks and advanced five thousand strong on Guadalupe Hill. The French general shouted, "It is twelve o'clock. Time to fight!"

Zaragoza, the Mexican general, commanded, "Charge the enemy!" It was then that both armies let their cannons roar.

The Mexicans were as fierce as fighting cocks against the French troops. It took only a moment for smoke to cover the sun. Shrieks and the terrible booms of the cannons filled the air.

Once, twice, three times the French tried to take the hill. Each time they were driven back.

In the end the French were no match for the Mexican army. Nor could they cope with the hills and ravines or the terrible storm. For the heavens opened that Cinco de Mayo, and a torrent of hailstones fell on the armies, soaking the gunpowder for the cannons.

The finest army in the world had to retreat, taking their fallen flag with them.

The battle lasted more than four hours.

On the fifth of May, 1862, the French were defeated. We won! And the French medals were lost in the dirt.

After the storm, it was calm. Now it was time to rest. On Guadalupe Hill there was silence.

But in San Miguel Tlaixpan there is joyful noise because no one has died in our battle. Frenchmen and Mexicans eat, sing and dance together.

Every year in our village we bring our heroes back to life. Zaragoza, Negrete, Juan Francisco and even Juarez the president are born again at our feast. And all of us — Mexicans, Frenchmen, Zacapoaxtle Indians and Chinacos — feel more alive than ever when we celebrate the Cinco de Mayo together.

This book is about the Battle of the Cinco de Mayo, an episode from the French intervention in Mexico.

Unfortunately, in history, encounters between peoples have often been warlike. Nonetheless, in time such events can sometimes take on a different meaning and become the occasion for myth and festivity. With time we can cease judging and begrudging, and turn our past into an opportunity for play. The battle at Puebla has become just such a legendary encounter.

In some Mexican villages these events are reenacted every year, with everyone playing the parts of the opposing forces and the village representing the setting for the battle. The photographs in this book were taken at a celebration in San Miguel Tlaixpan, in the State of Mexico. They have been combined with engravings that appeared in the French press at the time of the war. Two Mexican engravings are included at the end of the book; young readers will have fun discovering the differences between them.

The text is drawn from oral accounts of the participants in the modern-day festival. The historical account is based on war reports by generals in the Mexican army.

The Cinco de Mayo is much celebrated in the Mexican-American community, often without a knowledge of what the day means. By allowing us to understand why this event was so important, this book can help make our celebrations more meaningful.